Subnetting for Beginners:

How To Easily Master IP Subnetting And Binary Math To Pass Your CCNA

Contents

Introduction

I want to thank and congratulate you for purchasing the book *"Subnetting for Beginners"*

The Cisco CCNA exam is an IT Networking Certification Exam that tests what one knows about networking and switching. Part of the said exam is all about Subnetting, or the process of dividing identifier hosts to create subnets in the CIDR Notation Prefix.

It is an important part of the exam because it deals with IP addresses, which every device connected to a network has. With the help of this book, you'll become familiar with Subnetting — and get introduced to some activities and tests that will challenge your mind.

Should you choose to pursue your Cisco CCNA certification, when the day for the for your exam finally comes, you'll be able to answer those questions with full conviction and with the best of your knowledge and abilities.

Read this book now and learn more about Subnetting.

Once again, thank you and good luck!

Chapter 1: Subnetting Refresher Course

Let's get started with the basics!

Subnetting Basics

Basically, Subnetting deals with the process of having to divide networks into two or more smaller networks to create IP Network Subdivisions. The computers that would then belong to those divisions, apparently called *subnets,* have bitgroups that are almost identical in their IP addresses. This way, IP addresses would be logically divided and their addresses would have routing prefixes, with host identifiers that has something to do with the whole network. In short, *subnets* refer to *local organizations of connected network devices.*

The CIDR Notation, or Classless Inter-Domain Routing, also known as the method of routing Internet Protocols and allocating IP Addresses, replaced classful networks back in 1993 as the means to divide networks.

Classful designs came with IPV4 (8-bit addresses), while classless networks began to be introduced with IPV 6 that has 64 bits per convention. This is also the reason why IPV4 addresses seem to work slower than IPV6 addresses.

Traffic then gets to be exchanged between the networks or router gateways, with the router acting as the physical communication item between the two. With the help of subnetting, network management and routing efficiencies become better—especially in large organizations. Tree-routing structures also get to be partitioned, as well.

Please refer to the advantages of subnetting below.

Advantages of Subnetting

1. Subnetting helps you save money by making sure that IP Range Requirements are reduced.
2. Subnetting helps you apply network security policies when there is interaction between the subjects.
3. Subnetting removes collision so traffic is reduced, and the overall performance of the network is improved.
4. Subnetting breaks large networks down to smaller networks so they are easily managed.

How Do IP Addresses Work?

Now, it's also essential that you lknow how IP Addresses work, and what makes them what they are.

For starters, IP Addresses can be likened to Postal Addresses. While it is a series of numbers, each division defines specific geographical areas. IP Addresses are made up of two major bits, namely, the *network address* or *prefix*, and the *host identifier*—or the other numbers in the network. For example, the IP Address is something like this:

191.16.85.18

191 is the state of origin.

16 is the town.

38 is the house/apartment unit.

18 is the house/apartment number.

.

Intra-Subnets

Intra-Subnets are known as postal carrier switches where in the state of origin is considered domestic.

Let's say your IP Address is 192.168.8.1, but you sent something to 192.168.8.2. Obviously, what would happen is that the letter won't be able to reach the destination without the subnet mask. The mask acts as the messenger, and without it, your messages would just stay with you—and that is not really what you want to happen.

Chapter 2: Constructing IP/TCP Addresses

When it comes to the construction of IP/TCP Addresses, you need to deal with binaries and other logical numbers. Let's break the said numbers down so you'll easily understand them.

> **TCP/IP Addresses.** These consist of the whole 32-bit binary numbers that have then been converted into decimals.
>
> **Binary.** This is a number system that is based on zeroes and ones.
>
> **Bits.** Bits are then the term given to single characters. This means that 32-bit is equal to 32 ones or zeroes.
>
> **Octet.** As the name suggests, this is a group of 8 numbers. For example, if the IP Address is 192.168.1.1, the octets would be: 192, 168, 1, 1. Again, you have to keep in mind that we're talking about binaries here, not real numbers, so 8 is also equivalent to 4.

Now, for example, you have the IP Address 191.54.38.15. You can then convert it into binary this way:

Binaries

It would be good to know the basics of binaries first. For this, you have to keep in mind the following:

$$0001 = 1$$

$$0011 = 3$$

$$0110 = 6$$

$$1001 = 9$$

Each "1" is the representation of the power of 2. And then "0", of course, also resembles zero. This means that:

1 is 0001 because it is 2 to the power of zero.

2 is 0010 because it is 2 raised to the 1st power.

4 is 0100 because it is 2 raised to the 2nd power.

8 is 1000 because it is 2 raised to the 3rd power.

So basically, when you see 0101, it means that numbers have been raised to the power of 2. For this, you could keep in mind the following examples:

$$0 + 4 + 0 + 1 = 5 = 0101$$

$$8 + 0 + 2 + 0 = 10 = 1010$$

$$0 + 4 + 2 + 1 = 7 = 0111$$

Now, when you add two binaries together, you could get the following:

$$0001 + 0100 = 0101$$

$$0001 + 0001 = 0010$$

$$0011 + 0011 = 0110$$

$$0011 + 0101 = 1000$$

As for the larger numbers, you could take note of this guide:

$$0 = 0000$$

$$1 = 0001$$

$$2 = 0010$$

$$3 = 0011$$

$$4 = 0100$$

$$5 = 0101$$

$$6 = 0110$$

7 = 0111

8 = 1000

9 = 1001

10 = 1010

11 = 1011

12 = 1100

13 = 1101

14 = 1110

15 = 1111

And as for bigger binaries, you just have to have more bits.

Separating the Numbers

Then, keep in mind the Octets. Again, this is a group of 8 binaries. For the given example (**191.54.38.15**), For this you could do the following:

0/4 + ½ + 1/1 = 3

¼ + 0/2 + 1/1 = 4 (because binary is set to 100)

191 = 1011111

1/128 + 0/64 + 1/32 + 1/16 + 0/8 + ¼ + ½ + 0/1

For 54, you have 00110110, which means:

0/128 + 0/64 + 1/32 + 0/16 + 0/8 + ¼ + ½ + 0/1

For 38, the binary is 001001100, which means:

0/128 + 0/64 + 0/32 + 0/16 + 1/8 + ¼ + ½ + 1/1

For 15, the binary is 00001111, which gives you:

0/128 + 0/64 + 0/32 + 0/16 + 1/8 + ¼ + ½ + 1/1

So:

191 = 1011111

54 = 00110110

38 = 00100110

15 = 00001111

Is equal to:

191.54.38.15 and
10111111.00110110.00100110.00001111

There, you now have your complete octets.

0/128 + 0/64 + 0/32 + 0/16 + 1/8 + ¼ + ½ + 1/1

Subnet Masks

Next, you have your Subnet Masks that tell you where the network begins and ends. For this, you also have to convert the decimal numbers into binary because it covers the number of bits that are borrowed from the network's host component. You always should just go back to this concept every time you feel confused.

For this, the zeroes (0) will be the ones representing the hosts, while ones (1) represent the IP Network Portions.

For example, the IP Address is 192.168.1.0

You could then expect that this has a subnet mask of: 255.255.255.0

Now, you should convert the first octet into binary, which would then give you the following:

1/ 128

1/64

1/32

1/16

1/8

¼

½

11

Underneath the 1s you can add the numbers, and you'll see that you'd get the result of 255, which would then serve as your subnet mask.

Again, the subnet mask is 255.255.255.0. Once you convert this into binary, you'd get the result of:

11111111.11111111.11111111.00000000

The separation of 1s and 0s is then considered the *Network Boundary*, which would go something like this:

11111111.11111111.11111111.| **00000000**

So for that, you could say that the network is equivalent to the first three octets, while the host is deemed as the last octet. This means that:

192.168.1.0 is the *subnet*, and the hosts are:

192.168.1.0 up to 192.168.1.254

Take note that you'd get the number of hosts by taking the zero binaries to the power of two.

For the given example, you take 0s of 8s to the power of 2 where host is 2^n-2, n being the number of zeroes.

Suppose you have changed your subnet mask, you could start with this example:

192.168.1.0 is the IP Address, while 255.255.0.0 is the subnet mask. You already see the slight change, right? From 255.255.255.0, you now have 255.255.0.0.

The slash should then be used to determine the *network boundary*. So, for this one, it'll be like the one below:

11111111.11111111.|**00000000.00000000**

This will then give you:

192.168.0.0 as the subnet, and 192.168.0.1 up to 192.168.255.254 as the hosts.

Again, you'd get the number of hosts by taking the zero binaries to the power of two.

As for this example, you also have to take note that 192.168.0.0 cannot be considered as host because it is the address of the network itself, and 192.168.255.254 cannot be used as the broadcast address, but everything in the middle could be connected to the main address itself.

To help you understand this better, you might also want to keep in mind that IP Address and Subnet Mask both work in the bitwise And

Operation where a number or network address results in the subnet mask.

For this, you could keep in mind the following:

Class B IP Address is
10001100.10110011.11110000.11001000
140.179.240.200

Default Class C Subnet Mask is
11111111.11111111.00000000.00000000
255.255.000.000

Network Address is
10001100.10110011.00000000.0000000
0 140.179.000.000

Restrictive Masks

There are also more restrictive subnet masks where you get to add additional bits aside from what has already been given. This way, you could break the network down even more and create more subnets—but only if the internet connection could really supply everything with bandwidth. Otherwise, it really would just be a waste of time.

For this, you have to use the 2^N-2 formula where N is the number of bits in the field, and you have to raise 2 to the Nth power. This way, you'd get multiple nodes for your class. Mask bits for each subnet masks are not really recommended. Just take a look at the example below for clarity:

IP Address is 140.179.220.200
10001100.10110011.11011100.1100100

Subnet Mask is 255.255.224.000
11111111.11111111.11100000.00000000

Subnet Address is 140.179.192.000
10001100.10110011.11000000.0000000
0

Broadcast Address is 140.179.223.255
10001100.10110011.11011111.11111111

As you can see, the given example was able to use a 3-bit subnet mask—which isn't common for most of subnetting uses. It also used the 6 (2^3-2) formula because it's the only available formula for mask that is in this size.

This also means that you get a total of 49,140 nodes for the whole class—which is definitely a lot more than expected. You could also use the *Logical And Operation* for this, which means that the operations have to be done between two bits.

You could look at the "truth tables" for easy reference.

And

This is the result of 2 bits being compared. If these bits are both 1, automatically, the result would also be 1.

	0	1
0	0	0
1	0	1

XOR

This basically means Exclusive OR where 2 bits are compared, knowing that one of them is 1, even if they are in different values. Otherwise, the result would be zero.

	0	1
0	0	1
1	1	0

OR

OR is all about comparing 2 bits, which means that if both bits show the number 1, the automatic result is also 1. Otherwise, you could expect the result to be zero (0).

	0	1
0	0	1
1	1	1

NOT

This means that the value of a single digit could easily be changed. If you have 1, the result could be zero (o); if you have o, the result is 1. It is all about acting on a single digit, instead of comparing two bits.

0	1
1	0

Default Subnet Mask

It would be easier to subnet if you actually know default subnet masks that you could always rely on for each class. These are the following:

Class	Subnet Mask	Format
A	255.0.0.0	Network.Host.Host.Host
B	255.255.0.0	Network.Network.Host.Host
C	255.255.255.0	Network.Network.Network.Host

Subnetting Math

For more on Subnetting Math, you just have to keep in mind that binary math calculation is the main process you should keep in mind here. It's all about converting decimal to binary, and binary to decimal.

In a decimal system, you have a base number. Binary works the same as decimal system, with the exception of the said base number. To calculate this, just go ahead and use 2 as a replacement for the base value of 10. Again, remember that IP Addresses are made of 8 individual bits. Take a look at the table below for clarity.

Base Position	Decimal Value
2^7	128
2^6	64
2^5	32
2^4	16
2^3	8
2^2	4
2^1	2
2^0	0

In order to convert to binary, you have to make use of the addition method. Take note that if sum should be lower than the target number, and if so, you just have to keep adding. 1 bit will be added to the sum but it would still have the value of 0.

Let's say you want to convert the number 117 to binary. What would you do? Well, you could start with the table below.

Base Position	Decimal Value	Bit Statues	Decimal Value in Addition
2^7	128	0	0
2^6	64	1	64
2^5	32	1	32
2^4	16	1	16
2^3	8	0	0
2^2	4	1	4
2^1	2	0	0
2^0	0	1	1

Therefore, 117 becomes 01110101 when converted to binary.

Here's a calculated table for your convenience:

Decimal Calculation	Binary Bit
128 >117	Off bit
0 + 64 = 64 < 117	On bit
0 + 64 + 32 = 96 < 117	On bit
0 +64 + 32 + 16 = 112 < 117	On bit
0 + 64 + 32 + 16 + 8 = 120 > 117	Off bit
0 + 64 + 32 + 16 + 0 + 4 = 116 < 117	On bit
0 + 64 + 32 + 16 + 0 + 4 + 2 = 118 > 117	Off bit
0 + 64 + 32 + 16 + 0 + 4 + 0 + 1 = 117 = 117	On bit

Now, if you're going to convert binary into decimal, you have to keep in mind that you have to go from left all the way to the right.

For example, if you want to convert 10101010 into decimal, you have to follow the table below:

Base Position	Decimal Value	Bit Status	Decimal Value in Addition
2^7	128	1	128
2 ^6	64	0	0
2^5	32	1	32
2^4	16	0	0
2^3	8	1	8
2^2	4	0	0
2^1	2	1	2
2^0	0	0	0

Therefore, the decimal value of 10101010 is 170, because it is the sum total of the decimal values in addition.

To practice, just choose a number from 0 to 255 and try converting it into binary. Then, pick any combination from 00000000 to 11111111 and convert it to decimal. For reference, you could rely on this table below:

Binary Bit	Decimal Value
1 on bit	128
0 off bit	0
1 on bit	64
0 off bit	0
1 on bit	32
0 off bit	0
1 on bit	8
0 off bit	0
1 on bit	2
0 off bit	0

You could also learn more about combinations that are decided by the position of the binary.

For this, you can keep in mind what's on the table below.

Number of bits	Number of Combinations	Number of bits	Number of Combinations
1	2	17	131072
2	4	18	262144
3	8	19	524288
4	16	20	1048576
5	32	21	2097152
6	64	22	4194304
7	128	23	8388608
8	256	24	1677216
9	512	25	33554432
10	1024	26	67108864
11	2048	27	134217728
12	4096	28	268435456
13	8192	29	536870912
14	16384	30	1073741824
15	32768	31	2147483648
16	65536	32	4294967926

Subnet Mask Shorthand

Take note that instead of writing full subnets like 255.255.255.0, you could have them shortened to /24. For this, you need to make use of a Subnet Mask Chart—and sooner or later, you'll realize how helpful this could be!

Decimal	Shorthand	Binary
255.0.0.0	/8	11111111.00000000.00000000.00000000
255.128.0.0	/9	11111111.10000000.00000000.00000000
255.192.0.0	/10	11111111.11000000.00000000.00000000
255.224.0.0	/11	111111111.11100000.00000000.00000000
255.240.0.0	/12	11111111.11110000.00000000.00000000
255.248.0.0	/13	11111111.11111000.00000000.00000000
255.252.0.0	/14	11111111.11111100.00000000.00000000
255.254.0.0	/15	11111111.11111110.00000000.00000000
255.255.0.0	/16	11111111.11111111.00000000.00000000
255.255.128.0	/17	11111111.11111111.10000000.00000000
255.255.192.0	/18	11111111.11111111.11000000.00000000
255.255.244.0	/19	11111111.11111111.11100000.00000000

255.255.2 40.0	/20	11111111.11111111.11110000 . 00000000
255.255.2 48.0	/21	11111111.11111111.11111000 . 00000000
255.255.2 52.0	/22	11111111.11111111.11111100 . 00000000
255.255.2 54.0	/23	11111111.11111111.11111110. 00000000
255.255.2 55.0	/24	11111111.11111111.11111111. 00000000
255.255.2 55.128	/25	11111111.11111111.11111111. 10000000
255.255.2 55.192	/26	11111111.11111111.11111111. 11000000
255.255.2 55.224	/27	11111111.11111111.11111111. 11100000
255.255.2 55.240	/28	11111111.11111111.11111111. 11110000
255.255.2 55.248	/29	11111111.11111111.11111111. 11111000
255.255.2 55.252	/30	11111111.11111111.11111111. 11111100

You do not have to memorize the table above. Just copy and place it somewhere you can always see it while studying and while creating those subnets.

IP Address Classes

Now, you also have to take note that there are five IP Address Classes, and these are the following:

Class	Purpose	First Octet Range	Maximum Hosts	Total Networks
Class A	Extremely Large Networks	1 to 126*	16,777,216(2^{24})	128 (2^7)
Class B	Large Enterprises	128 to 191	65,536 (2^{16})	16,384 (2^{14})
Class C	Small Business	192 to 233	256 (2^8)	2,097,152 (2^{21})
Class D	Multicast	224 to 339	N/A	N/A
Class E	Experimental	240 to 255	N/A	N/A

Take note that the asterisk (*) means that digits between 0 to 127 are reserved for certain functions.

You could also make use of the following binaries:

Class A = 0

Class B = 10

Class C = 110

Class D = 1110

Class E = 1111

Private Network Ranges

Now, you have to remember that each of these classes also have their corresponding Private Ranges so that IP Addresses could be conserved. This means that you can substitute real IP Addresses so communication would be easy, no matter the number of hosts there are.

For this, just keep the following in mind:

Class A Private Addresses always begin with the number 10, with the following binary: 10.0.0.0/8

Class B Private Addresses begin with 172.16 up to 31, with the following binary: 172.16.0.0/12

Class C Private Addresses begin with 192.168 with the following binary:

192.168.0.0/16

Subnet Zero

Take note that once upon a time, using zero with the first network was considered bad practice mainly because it would not be used.

However, with Cisco, Zero is considered okay— so when you have ranges like 192.168.1.0 to 192.168.1.9, you can definitely use it, especially when taking the exam and you see that the subnet zero command has been turned on.

Reserved Host Addresses

Again, take note that for each address that has been created, the first and last addresses are reserved. For this, you have to keep the following in mind:

Network ID is the *first IP Address.*

Broadcast Address is the *last IP Address.*

So, basically, you could put the following examples in mind:

192.168.1.1 = IP Address

255.255.255.0 = Subnet Mask

192.168.1.0 = Network ID

192.168.1.255 = Broadcast Address

192.168.1.1 to 192.168.1.254 = Useful IP Addresses

Chapter 3: VLSM and Route Summarization

VLSM

VLSM is the term given to Variable Length Subnet Mask.

For example, you are the administrator of a network and that you're tasked to set up the IP Network, with only a single Class C IP Address Range. This means you would have to set up these networks that you see below:

100 hosts = Network A

40 hosts = Network B

20 hosts = Network C

10 hosts = Network D

6 hosts = Network E

2 hosts = Network F

This means that you have to add all the host requirements together to get a single block. Then, work from the top all the way to the bottom. Make sure to remove the network's required hosts, as well.

To understand this better, take a look at the table below:

IP Range	Network	Num IPs	Subnet Mask
0 to 127	Network A	128	/25
128 to 191	Network B	64	/26
192 to 223	Network C	32	/27
224 to 239	Network D	16	/28
240 to 247	Network E	8	/29
248 to 251	Network F	4	/30

Route Summarization

Basically, this is all about increasing a router's performance by making use of a summarized route. The great thing about summarized routes is that it reduces traffic and limits route table.

Here's a good example. Suppose you have 4 different LANs attached to your router. For this, you would have:

192.168.0.0/24 = Network A

192.168.1.0/24 = Network B

192.168.2.0/24 = Network C

192.168.3.0/24 = Network D

To summarize all these, you first would have to convert the IP addresses to binary and write them down in a table, like the one shown below:

Decimal	Binary
192.168.0.0	11000000.10101000.00000000.00000000
192.168.1.0	11000000.10101000.00000001.00000000
192.168.2.0	11000000.10100000.00000010.00000000
192.168.3.0	11000000.10100000.00000011.00000000

Now, go ahead and count the common bits from the left all the way to the right of the table. Since you could see that the first two octets are pretty much the same, and that there are also similarities with the first 8 bits of the octet. This means you could just draw a line to figure out the changes.

Then, go and count the mask's common bits. Since we have 22 bits in the example, you could conclude that 192.168.0.0/22 is the answer.

Here's another example:

10.10.0.0/16 = Network 1

10.11.0.0/16 = Network 2

10.12.0.0/16 = Network 3

10.13.0.0/16 = Network 4

10.14.0.0/16 = Network 5

10.15.0.0/16 = Network 6

To see this in binary, you can refer to the table below:

Decimal	Binary
10.10.0.0	00001010.00001010.00000000.00000000
10.11.0.0	00001010.00001011.00000000.00000000
10.12.0.0	00001010.00001100.00000000.00000000
10.13.0.0	00001010.00001101.00000000.00000000
10.14.0.0	00001010.00001110.00000000.00000000
10.15.0.0	00001010.00001111.00000000.00000000

This means that the first five bits of the first octet are identical. Therefore, 8 + 5 = 13, which means that the answer is 10.8.0.0/13 because 8 has been derived from a block of 8.

Chapter 4: Important Terminologies

To make the process of reviewing easier, it would be helpful to keep important subnet terminologies in mind. You'll find them all in this chapter!

Subnet

Subnet shares the same address as its other components. On IP Addresses, it is determined by the same prefixes especially on TCP/IP Networks.

For example, devices that work in the IP Address 192.168.8.1 mean that they are the part of the same subnet. This is important for both performance and security reasons.

Subnet Mask

The Subnet Mask determines the subnet where the IP Address belongs to, which also deals with the host and network address.

As a review, for the address 150.215.017.009, you have 150.215 as part of one class (Class B), and 017.009 as the host.

Say, the network is divided into 14 subnets, you can expect that the bits will be reserved for a subnetwork that could be considered as an identifying network.

Decimal

Decimal refers to the numbers found in Base 10 (which are basically numbers used in one's day-to-day life). These are the following numbers:

9

100345000

-256

Mask

Mask is the term given to an item that identifies the subnet itself by performing the *bitwise And Operation*.

It also could include and exclude certain values. You could have the mask assigned to something that cannot be entered or conformed to.

Bit

This is the smallest given unit in a machine that can hold only 2 values, which are zero (0), and one (1).

Bit is the short term for Binary Digit.

Bitwise

Bitwise is known as an operator that can manipulate each and every bit. It works with bytes and other operators to support programming languages. Examples include:

<<<< Shifts bits left

>>>> Shifts bits right

~ Compliments a group of bits

^ Creates XOR compare on two bit groups

| Creates OR compare on two bit groups

& Creates AND compare on two bit groups

Take note though that these could not be used for ALL programming languages.

And Operation

This returns the TRUE value if both operands are TRUE. Otherwise, it would be FALSE.

Variable Length Subnet Mask

This is also known as VLSM and is the term given for another subnet mask in the same network. Basically, long subnets could be used for this, with the blessing of the network operator. Take note that Routing Protocol is important for this to happen.

Routing

Routing is also known as Internetworking and is known as the process of transporting packet data from its source all the way to its destination with the help of a router.

This is one of the internet's key features because it allows the process of communication to be prevalent with computers and networks. Sometimes, routes are also analyzed to make sure that a message (re: an email, a tweet, etc) reaches its destination.

However, you should not have this confused with *bridging,* which gives almost the similar function. Bridging always happens at lower levels and mostly works on hardware, instead of software. It also cannot handle complex operations the way routing could.

Protocol

Protocol is the term given to the format of transporting data that has been agreed upon by all parties involved. It is able to make light of the following:

1. The method of data compression (if applicable);
2. The type of data error checker that has been used;
3. The indicator that shows a data has been sent;
4. The indicator that shows a data has been received.

Programmers can choose from a variety of protocols, depending on their programming language and on the software they are trying to make. The said protocol can then be implemented whether in software or hardware.

Data Compression

Data Compression is the process of storing data in a larger space than normal. This is mostly used in communication protocols because it allows devices to store or emit data in a manner that is far better than standardized, especially when modems are around.

Key Length

Key Length is the term given to the number of bits or binary digits in an encryption. It is also used to measure the encryption algorithm's relative strength.

Fixed Length

As the name suggests, this is a binary length that stays the same no matter what happens. It could also refer to the entire record.

Focal Length

Just like in photography, focal length is known as the size and angle of the filed onscreen the way you can view it.

Subnet Calculator

This is basically used to compute subnets automatically.

With a subnet calculator, you will be able to type in an IP Address and choose the corresponding Subnet Mask and Network Class, together with other variables needed to complete the operation.

You will then get a hexadecimal IP Address once you have already computed everything. You would also be given the Wildcard ID, Broadcast Address, and Subnet ID, as well.

APIPA (Automatic Private IP Addressing)

APIPA could be found in recent versions of the Windows Operating System which allows IP Addresses to self-configure with the help of DHCP Clients, even if a server is not available.

Once the client has booted up, it will be able to obtain an IP Address and a Subnet Mask by looking for its own server.

However, if it cannot find the needed information, APIPA will then automatically configure itself from a range that has been reserved for Microsoft. This range could be 169.254.0.1 to 169.254.255.254. A Class B Subnet Mask could also be used for configuration once the DHCP Address becomes readily available.

This is usually meant for small businesses with only 25 clients and that are in non-routed environments.

Client

Client is an important part of the Client-Server Architecture that usually runs on a workstation or a personal computer and needs a server in order to perform certain operations.

One good example is an email client (i.e., *Gmail, Yahoo*, etc.) which is known as such because it allows you to send and receive emails.

Host

A host is known as a computer system that could be accessed by the user. This is usually used when there are two computer systems around that have been connected by telephone lines and modems. It also contains the data.

A host can also be something that provides a computer system with its own infrastructure. For example, it could be one of those companies that host applications, programs, and files for individuals and companies in a web server. It also provides both software and hardware with the right attributes.

And finally, a host could also be considered as something that is connected to the TCP/IP Network, with a unique IP Address, and which includes the internet, in general.

DHCP

DHCP is also known as Dynamic Host Configuration Protocol which is responsible for assigning IP Addresses to a given network.

When this happens, different IP Addresses could work with only one device every single time that it connects to the network. These addresses could also change even while they are still connected to the system. It could also work for both dynamic and static addresses, and is also able to simplify network administration. This is because it tracks IP Addresses itself, instead of looking for an administrator who could track the said addresses. It means that DHCP could save both time and effort for the user.

IP Address (Internet Protocol)

The IP Address acts as the identifier for devices/computers working in the IP/TCP System, and that go under the Protocol Route.

It specifies Packet Formats that are also known as datagrams, while addressing the problems of the protocol itself.

The format is always a 32-bit number written as 4 numbers that are separated by periods. This could go from 0 to 255 and could even be assigned at random, provided the numbers are really unique.

In order to view your own IP Address, you could try using the *command line* tool. Input *ipconfig (IPCONFIG)* and you will get the configuration that you need. Make sure to refresh the system before doing so.

Static IP Address

This is an address that will never change no matter what happens.

Dynamic IP Address

This is only a temporary IP Address that gets assigned to the device or computer every time it connects online.

TCP/IP – Transmission Control Protocol/ Internet Protocol

This is pretty much known as the base of all internet protocols that allows hosts to connect to the internet. With this comes several protocols, with IP/TCP as the main ones.

This has been originally built to the UNIX System, which made it the prime communication line of internet network systems.

Virtual IP Address

This is a Virtual IP Address that is shared in various domain names working on multiple servers. This also takes away the host's dependency on individual interfaces with packets that are sent to the original system, but also travel through various networks.

Dynamic NAT

This is a private IP Address that has been drawn from a pool of registered IP Addresses. Usually, it is the only router that works in a network that keeps track of registered IP Addresses.

What usually happens is that the internet chooses an address that is not often used—even if it has been around for a long time. This may be one of those free addresses that have been left without any activity for a while, so in order for it to be useful again, it becomes a Dynamic NAT.

What's also great about this is that it allows private addresses to work as internal addresses—so nothing really gets wasted.

Internet Address

This is the term given to nodes found on the internet. This may also be the term given to a website's IP, and could also represent one's email address.

Node

A node is the processing location of a network, which can also be found in a computer, printer, or in other related devices. Take note that each node has a unique address and that sometimes, it's also called Media Access or Data Link Control Address.

Loopback Address

127.0.0.1 is known as the Loopback Address. It is considered to be a special IP number that is connected to the loopback of a machine or a server itself. Take note that no hardware is and should be associated with it.

What makes the Loopback Address essential is the fact that it allows IT Professionals to go ahead and test the software that they have used. This way, the user would not have to worry about broken hardware or corrupted drivers.

Address Bar Spoofing

This is the result of malicious software where the browser bar forces the original browser to display webpages that has been chosen by the attacker or hacker. This replaces the original address with something fake and that's why you have to beware of it.

Martian Address

The Martian Address is an invalid IP Address that has been spoofed because of the fact that it is not routable, and has been placed in a system that's been misconfigured. Any kind of Routing Software will reject this kind of address.

Chapter 5: Subnetting Reminders and Tips

Before you create a Subnetting Cheat Sheet and before you check various questions that you could practice on before the exam, it would be good to remind yourself of certain guidelines that are important while subnetting.

Read on and find out what they are!

CIDR

Here's what you need to remember about the number of bits in one network address:

1. Class A should be written as a slash notation of /8 because it has a default subnet mask of 255.0.0.0, with the first octet having mask in all of the bits.

2. Class B should be written as a slash notation of /16 because it has a default subnet mask of 255.255.0.0 which means masks are contained in all bits of the first octet.

3. Class C should be written as a slash notation of /24 because it has a default subnet mask of 255.255.255.0 with all bits on the first three octets.

It would also be easier to understand CIDR Notation if you could arm yourself with the proper table for reference, just like the one below:

CIDR	Decimal	Binary
/25	128	10000000
/26	192	11000000
/27	224	11100000
/28	240	11110000
/29	248	11111000
/30	252	11111100

Questions to Ask before Subnetting

There are certain questions you have to ask yourself before you begin to subnet. These are:

1. What is the broadcast address of each subnet?

The answer mainly is that the last address of the subnet is considered as the broadcast address. This is reserved for the whole network broadcast, and cannot be used by any other hosts—even if it is assigned to them. For example:

63 is the broadcast address of 0 subnet.

127 is the broadcast address of 67 subnet.

191 is the broadcast address of 68 subnet.

255 is the broadcast address of 192 subnet.

2. How many valid hosts are available per subject?

The key element here is to reduce 2 addresses for each of the subnets –one for the broadcast ID, and one for the network ID. Now, you can call something a valid host if it is one of those assigned to the devices.

If you have 2 valid devices, it means you have 2 valid hosts. So, if you have 48 hosts per subnet, you have to take away 2, and the answer is that you have 46 valid hosts!

3. What are the total hosts?

Total hosts mean that they are the number of hosts available for each subnet.

If you need to calculate for the number of hosts, you have to use the formula 2^H = total hosts, with H declaring the number of host bits.

Let's say the IP Address is 192.168.1.0/26. Compute by subtracting the bits consumed by the network address from the total bits in the IP Address. In this case, that would be 32-26, which means that you have 6 as the total number of hosts.

4. What are the valid subnets?

The valid subnets are calculated by means of a two-step process.

For this, you first have to compute for the total subnet by using the 2^N formula until you reach the value of the subnet mask.

Let's say your IP Address is 192.168.1.0/26, for this, you'd have:

26-64 = 2 (borrowed host bits)

Count from zero until you reach blocks of 64 (64, 128. 256, etc).

Block size would be 64. (256-192)

Subnet Mask would be 255.255.255.192

Finally, total subnets are 4 (2^2)

5. What is the block size for the subnet mask?

The block size is the increment used to compute for the valid subnets. Basically, you can figure out what the subnets are if you know what the block size is.

If your IP Address is 192.168.1.0/27, you can determine that 3 is N and that it belongs to Class C. For this, you have the default subnet mask of 255.255.255.0, with 1/24 CIDR.

Borrow 24 from 27 and you'd have the amount of 3, Now, go ahead and raise 2 to the 3rd power and you'd get the answer of 8.

Therefore, your block size is 8.

6. How many subnets does the given subnet mask provide?

For this, one you have to use the 2^N formula, where N stands for the borrowed bits from the host bits.

Again, if the IP Address is 192.168.1.0, you could say that N is 3 and that it belongs to Class C with the default subnet mask of 255.255.255.0 or 1/24 in CIDR.

7. What is the subnet mask for the given address?

Well, this always depends on the given address.

However, you have to keep in mind that subnetting is all about how the default subnet mask could be extended—and it would always help if you could write down the default subnet mask.

For example, the IP Address is 188.25.45.48/20. This means that the address is categorized in Class B and that it has the default subnet mask of 255.255.0.0/16, and therefore, you'd be able to borrow 4 bits from the host.

Move from left to right and you'll get the binary of 111111111.111111111.11110000.00000000 with the first two octets being the default value, and with the third octet being converted into decimals.

For this, you have to use the equation: 128 + 64 + 32 + 16 + 0 + 0 + 0 +0 = 240.

Therefore, your subnet mask will be 255.255.240.0

8. What is the network address of each subnet?

Take note that the network address is the subnet's first address and is always used to locate the network. Take note that this could not be assigned to just about any host.

For example, you have 0, 64, 128, and 192 as the network address. For this, you have to keep the following in mind:

> Valid hosts are those IP Addresses that are between the broadcast and network address.

> The last IP Address of the subnet is considered as the broadcast address.

> The first IP Address of the subnet is known as the network address.

Final Reminders before Subnetting

Here are some of those tips that you need to keep in mind before subnetting:

1. Subnet bits always start at the left all the way to the right. Be careful not to skip bits.

2. Network ID and Broadcast ID have to be reversed regardless of how many bits are left in the host field.

3. Do not assign the Network ID to a Broadcast ID for hosting.

4. When bits have already been assigned, there is no way for them to be changed—no matter what network class it is in.

5. There is a predefined subnet mask for each network class. This will help you learn more about the octets and what kind they are. This will also help you know how many more bits are available to work with.

6. There is also a predefined IP Class for each Network Address and this also cannot be changed.

7. There are at least 8 bits for a 32-bit IP Address and these belong to the same portion of a network, with at least 2 bits in the host portion.

8. The two packets in the two network bits are intended for different networks.

9. A subnet is always the smaller portion of one large network—and you do have to borrow bits from the portion of the host and have them assigned to the network.

Chapter 6: Creating a Subnetting Cheat Sheet

It would be good to create a Subnetting Cheat Sheet because then, you'd easily be able to solve subnetting problems without having a hard time. Here's a good way to do it.

First, you have to create a table with 3 columns and 14 rows, like the one you'll see below.

Now, go ahead and label the columns with *Bit, Exponent/Block Size*, and *Decimal Mask Value*.

Bits	Exponents/Block Size	Decimal Mask Value

Now, count from 1 to 12 in the column labeled *Bits,* and place those numbers on the table.

Bits	Exponents/Block Size	Decimal Mask Value
0		
1		
2		
3		
4		
5		
6		
7		

8		
9		
10		
11		
12		

Then, for the Exponent/Block Size Column, start with the number 1. For the succeeding numbers, double each of the preceding numbers until you reach the end of the column.

Bits	Exponents/Block Size	Decimal Mask Value
0	1	255
1	2	254
2	4	252
3	8	248
4	16	240
5	32	224
6	64	192
7	128	128
8	256	
9	512	
10	1024	
11	2048	
12	4096	

This now means that one octet is represented by the numbers 0 to 7. The remaining, shaded rows could then be able to determine other exponents when 2 is raised to the power of 10 or 11.

In the next chapter, you'll be able to practice what you have learned with the help of certain tests! Check them out, and check your knowledge.

Chapter7: Subnet Cheat Sheet Review Questions

Question 1

What is the Network ID, First Usable IP, Broadcast Address, or Last Usable IP on the subnetwork that the 192.168.1.15/26 node belongs to?

Solution

1. Convert the shorthand to a decimal value. Basically, it would be like this:

> /26 = 255.255.255 plus another 2 subnet bits

> Look at the cheat sheet and then count up from 128 by twos. This way, you'd get 192.

This now means that the subnet mask is 255.255.255.192!

2. Now, go ahead and determine the block size. For this one, it will be 64.

3. Determine the Network ID. For this, you have: 192.168.1.0

4. Find out what the next Network ID is. For this, you could do the following:

Check the 64 block size, and you'll figure out that 192.168.1.64 is the next Network ID.

192.168.1.0 is the main Network ID.

192.168.1.63 is the Broadcast ID.

192.168.1.1 is the first usable ID.

192. 168.1.62 is the last usable ID.

Now, here's another variation of this. What is the Network ID, First Usable IP, Broadcast Address, or Last Usable IP on the subnetwork that the 172.30.118.230/23 node belongs to?

To compute, here's what you have to do:

1. Convert shorthand to decimal.

/23 = 255.255 + seven more bits

Count seven from 128 in the cheat sheet to get 254.

This means that the decimal subnet is 255.255.254.0

2. Now, determine the block size by checking the block size in the cheat sheet. For this, it is 2.

3. To figure out what your Network ID is, remember that you are working in the third octet

with 2 as the block size. This means that the first network is 172.30.118.0, because 2 has been multiplied by 59 to get the result of 118.

4. Now, to determine the next Network ID, just go and do the following:

> Remember that the block size of 2 would yield the result that the next network is 172.30.120.0
>
> 172.30.118.0 is the Network ID.
>
> 172.30.119.255 is the Broadcast Address.
>
> 172.30.118.1 is the first usable ID.
>
> 172.30.119.254 is the last usable ID.

Question 2

Say you have the network 192.168.1.0 with the subnet mask 255.255.255.244. How many subnets and hosts per subnets could you get from it?

Solution

1. For this one, you have to determine what the classful mask is. For this, you have:

> Class C = 192
>
> 255.255.255.0 = default mask

2. Now, try to see how many more subnet bits will exist beyond the boundary. For this one, you just have to look at the 4th octet. You'll see that 224 is the decimal mask, so basically you can conclude that there are 3 subnets for this one.

3. Now, understand how many more bits there are. If there are 3 bits that have been seen earlier, you can conclude that you now have 5 more host bits.

4. Then, check the exponents of host and subnet bits. For this, you'd have:

$2\char`^3 = 8$ (subnet bits)

$2\char`^5\text{-}2 = 30$ (host bits)

So the answer for this question is that you have 8 subnets, and each of those subnets have 30 hosts.

Question 3

The next question is this: Say you have been asked to create a subnet mask for the network 172.16.0.0. You've been told that 900 subnets are needed for your organization, and that there should be at least 50 hosts for each subnet. The question is, which subnet mask should you be using?

Solution

1. For this one, you first have to know how many subnet bits there are so that you'd be able to cover the number of needed subnets. So, basically:

> You have to know that Class B was the given address, which means that there are 16 static subnet bits.

> Find the exponent of 2 in the cheat sheet, and make sure that it is greater than the 900 required subnets. This means you'd get 1,024 subnets with 10 additional subnet bits. You'll also see that 255.255.255.192 is the subnet mask.

> Now, you'd also see that there are eight ones (1s) in the third octet, and that there are two ones (1s) in the 4th. Count from the bottom of the sheet and you will get 192.

> Then, make sure that you confirm that the remaining amount of zeroes will be able to cover the number of required hosts. You have 6 zeroes now, and $2^6-2=62$. This means the zeroes could really cover everything and are actually more than enough.

2. Therefore, you'd know that 255.255.255.192 is your subnet mask. You also have 1024 subnets and 62 hosts for each subnet.

Chapter 8: Subnetting Multiple Choice

Connecting Hosts A & B

Say there are hosts A and B that the administrator is trying to connect through the Ethernet. (You'll see an illustration below) Now, you have tried to ping the hosts but apparently, it was unsuccessful. The question is, what can you do to make sure that the hosts get to be connected?

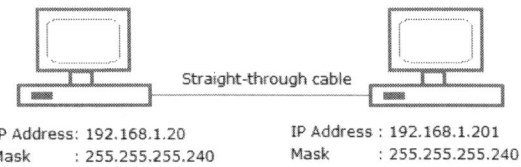

Straight-through cable

IP Address: 192.168.1.20
Mask   : 255.255.255.240

IP Address : 192.168.1.201
Mask   : 255.255.255.240

Options:

1. There should be a crossover cable instead of a straight-through cable.

2. Instead of the straight-through cable, there should be a rollover cable.

3. 255.255.255.192 should be set as the subnet mask.

4. Each host should have their own default gateway.

5. 255.255.255.0 should be set as the subnet mask.

Choices:

A. 1

B. 2

C. 3 and 4

D. 1 and 5

E. 2 and 5

Answer

The Answer for this question is D, or Options 1 and 5. This means that there should be a crossover cable instead of straight-through cable, and that subnet mask should be 255.255.255.0.

This so happens because if you really want to connect the hosts, you definitely should have a cable with you. However, it's obvious that straight-through cables won't work because the hosts do not have similar masks. So, what you can do is get a crossover cable, and then set masks to 255.255.255.0/24.

Valid Hosts and LAN Interface

Suppose your Ethernet's IP Address is 0: 172.16.2.1/23, What do you think would be the right LAN Interface ID when it's attached to the router?

Options:

1. 172.16.1.100

2. 172.16.1.198

3. 172.16.2.255

4. 172.16.3.0

Choices:

A. 1

B. 2 and 3

C. 3 and 4

D. None of the Above

Answer
The answer for this question is C, or both 172.16.2.255 and 172.16.3.0.

You have to see it this way: The IP Address on the router is 172.16.2.1/23 which is the address on the EO Interface, with subnet mask of 255.255.254.0. This then means that 2 is the size of the third octet.

Now, 2.0 subnet is the router's interface and it has the address of 3.255 because you have 4.0 as the next subject. So, 2.1 to 3.254 is the valid host range, making the router the first valid host here.

The 5 Subnets

You're asked to have a subnet network containing 5 subnets, with 16 hosts in each of them. The question is, which subnet mask should you use?

Choices:

A. 255.255.255.192

B. 255.255.255.224

C. 255.255.255.240

D. 255.255.255.248

Answer

For this, the answer is B, or 255.255.255.224.

Again, you need 16 hosts for each of your five subnets. The other subnets mentioned would give 14, 8, and 30 hosts, so obviously, your much needed subnet is 255.255.255.224.

Maximum Number of IP Addresses

If the subnet mask used in a local subnet is 255.255.255.224, how many number of IP Addresses could be assigned to it?

Choices:

A. 14

B. 15

C. 16

D. 30

Answer

D, or 30 is the maximum number of IP Addresses you could assign to the given subnet because the subnet is 3 bits on and 3 bits off. A, B, and C would not do anything for you.

Choosing Statements

The IP Address 10.16.3.65/23 is defined by which two statements?

Options:

1. 10.16.3.0 255.255.254.0 is the subnet address.

2. 10.16.2.1 255.255.254.0 is the lowest host address in the given subnet.

3. 10.16.2.254 255.255.254.0 is the last valid host address in the given subnet.

4. 10.16.3.254 255.255.254.0 is the subnet's broadcast address.

Choices:

A. 1 and 3

B. 2 and 4

C. 1, 2, and 4

D. 2, 3, and 4

Answer

The answer for this question is B, or .16.2.1 255.255.254.0 is the lowest host address in the given subnet, and 10.16.3.254 255.255.254.0 is the subnet's broadcast address.

This is because the Class A Address has a mask of 255.255.254.0/23, which gives you 9 host bits for 15 subnets, with 2 as the block size for the third octet. This means that the octet would be 0, 2, 4, 6 until 254 because the 2.0 subject has the host 10.16.3.65, with the next valid subnet as 4.0.

Finally, you have valid addresses between 2.1 to 3.254.

Number of Subnets and Hosts

172.16.0.0/19 has how many subnets and hosts?

Choices:

A. 7 subnets with 30 hosts

B. 8 subnets with 8,190 hosts

C. 8 subnets with 2,046 hosts

D. 7 subnets with 2,076 hosts

Answer

The answer for this question is B, or 8 subnets and 8,190 hosts.

This is because /19 has the CIDR address of 255.255.224.0, which means that this is a Class B Address and that there are only 3 subnet bits with 8 subnets, 13 host bits, and of course 8,190 hosts.

Subnetwork of a Host

The next question is: If you have an IP Address of 172.16.66.0/21, then what is your subnetwork number?

Choices:

A. 172.16.36.0

B. 172.16.48.0

C. 172.16.64.0

D. 172.16.0.0

Answer
For this, the answer is C because you have a block size of 8 in the third octet, with A/21 255.255.248.0. So what you can do here is count to 8 up until you reach 66, with subnet 64.0, and with the next one as 72.0 so you'd get 71.255 as the broadcast address.

Ethernet Subnet Address
Suppose an IP Address of 176.16.112.1/25 has been assigned to your Ethernet Port, the valid subnet address would be?

Choices:

A. 172.16.112.0

B. 172.16.0.0

C. 172.16.96.0

D. 172.16.255.0

Answer
The answer for this one is A since 255.255.255.128 with a mask of A/25.

This means that the third and fourth octets are used in the Class B network that makes a total of 9 subnet bits, with 1 bit in the 4th octet and 8 bits in the 3rd octet. This means that the bit could either be on or off, which gives it the value of either 128 or 0.

For this, you could broadcast with 127 or 128 with 0 subnet.

The 29 Subnets

Suppose you need 29 subnets for your network, and you need to create this while being able to maximize each of the subnet addresses. The question is, what number of bits should you borrow to provide the right subnet mask?

Choices:

A. 2

B. 3

C. 4

D. 5

Answer

The answer for this question is D.

This is because you have 16 subnets for 4 subnet bits in a 240 mask—which means you do have to add more subnet bits. This, in turn means that a 248 mask would give you one more subnet bit, and that 32 subnet bits are needed for 5 subnets, with 6 hosts per subnet.

Interface on Router

Suppose you have an IP Address of 192.168.192.10/29. How many hosts could be assigned with IP Addresses including the router interface, with the LAN attached to the interface?

Choices:

A. 6

B. 8

C. 30

D. 32

Answer

The answer for this is A, because there are only 3 host bits regardless of class address for A/29 (255.255.255.248), which means 6 would be the maximum number of hosts on the LAN—router interface included.

IP Stack on the Local Host
Which IP Address should you ping if you want to test IP Stack on your local host?

Choices:

A. 127.0.0.0

B. 1.0.0.127

C. 127.0.0.1

D. 127.0.0.255

Answer
The answer here is C, because you have to ping loopback of 127.0.0.1 if you want to test your local network.

Mask on the VLSM Network
Which mask should you use on your WAN, point-to-point, if you want to reduce IP Address waste?

Choices:

A. /27

B. /28

C. /29

D. /30

Answer

The answer here is D.

This is because there are only 2 hosts for the point-to-point WAN which are either 255.255.255.252, or A/30, which provides the said number of hosts per subject.

Valid Host Address

What is the valid host address if 172.16.17.0/22 is the subnet of your network?

Choices:

A. 172.16.17.1 255.255.255.252

B. 172.16.0.1 255.255.240.0

C. 172.16.20.1 255.255.254.0

D. 172.16.18.255 255.255.252.0

Answer

For this, your best choice is option D.

This is because /22 mask has 4 block size in the third octet, with subnet 255.255.252.0. Since the subnet of your network address is 172.16.16.0, you'd know that 172.16.18.255 is the only valid host for this question.

Broadcast Address on the LAN

Say your IP Address is 192.168.192.10/29 and that it has interface on a router. What do you think should the hosts of the LAN use as broadcast address for this one?

Choices:

A. 192.168.192.15

B. 192.168.192.31

C. 192.168.192.33

D. 192.168.192.127

Answer

For this, the answer is A, or 192.168.192.15 because its 4th octet has the block size of 8. It also has the mask of 255.255.255.248 in the A/29 octet, with the subnets of 0, 8, 16, 24, and as follows.

The next subnet would then either be 15 or 16, which makes A the right choice.

Configuring a Server

You're asked to configure a server with subnet 192.168.19.24/29, with the first available host address being the router. Which of the following numbers should you then assign to the server?

Choices:

A. 192.168.19.0 255.255.255.0

B. 192.168.19.33 255.255.255.240

C. 192.168.19.26   255.255.255.248

D. 192.168.19.31   255.255.255.248

Answer

The answer for this is C.

This is because there are 8 blocks for the 4th octet of 255.255.255.248 in A/29 with subnets of 0. 8, 16, 24, 32, 40, and so on.

Therefore, you'd realize that the subnet is 192.168.19.24 with 24 being the subnet. Now, you have 32 as the next subnet with broadcast address of 24, which means that only 192.168.19.26 255.255.255.248 could be considered the right answer.

EO IP Address

Look at the illustration below and figure out what the IP Address of EO should be, if you are currently using the 8th subnet. Use the last available IP Address of the ID 192.168.10.0/28. Zero is not a valid subnet for this equation.

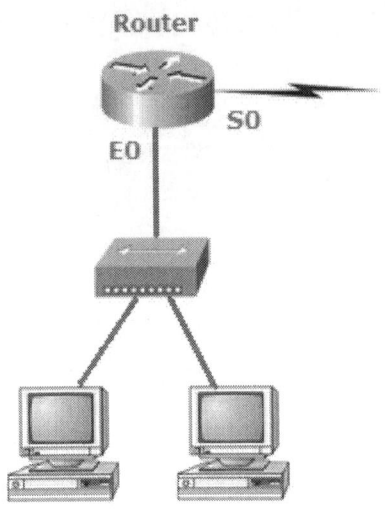

Router

S0

E0

Choices:

A. 192.168.10.142

B. 192.168.10.66

C. 192.168.100.254

D. 192.168.10.143

E. 192.168.10.126

Answer

For this question, your best answer would be A, or 192.168.10.142 as it has the subnet mask of 255.255.255.240 in A/28.

Now, go and count up to the 9th subnet starting from 16 to figure out what the broadcast address is. Now, make sure that you count 8s, starting with 16, 32, 48, 64, 80, 112, and so on with the 8th subnet being 128, and the next one being 144, which means that broadcast address is 143 and host range is between 129 to 142, with 142 being the last valid host.

Subnetwork of a Host 2

Say that the host network belongs to the IP Address 172.16.45.14/30. The question is, which subnetwork does this host belong to?

Choices:

A. 172.16.45.0

B. 172.16.45.4

C. 172.16.45.8

D. 172.16.45.12

Answer

The answer for this question is D, because regardless of class, it is A/30 with 4th octet being 252. This also means that the subnets would be 0, 4, 8, 12, and 16 with block size of 4, and 14 being on then 12th subnet.

Subnetwork Address

Suppose the IP Address is 200.10.5.68/28, what do you think is the subnetwork address for the host?

Choices:

A. 200.10.5.56

B. 200.10.5.32

C. 200.10.5.64

D. 200.10.5.0

Answer

For this, the answer would be C, mostly because it has the subnet mask of 255.255.255.240 in A/28.

This means that the 4th octet has a block size of 16, and follows the hosts 0, 16, 32, 48, 64, and so on, with 64 being the subnet.

SO IP Address

Again, look at the illustration below. You'll notice it's the same as an earlier example. Now, the question here is what do you think would the SO IP Address would be if the network ID is 192.168.10.0/28. Take note that you're asked to use the last available IP from the range, and that zero would not be considered a subnet.

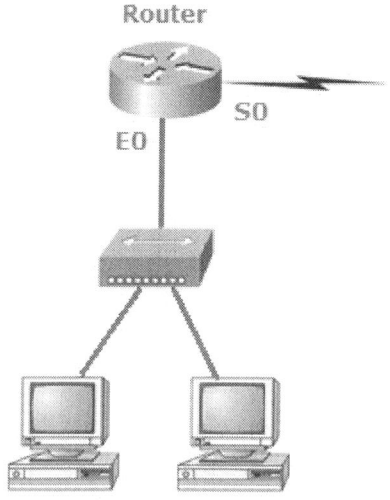

Choices:

A. 192.168.10.24

B. 192.168.10.62

C. 192.168.10.30

D. 192.168.10.127

Answer

For this, the answer would be C. This means that you have a mask of 255.255.255.240 in A/28 with 16 as the first subnet, and 32 being the next subnet, which gives you the broadcast address of 31.

This means that 30 is the last valid host from a range of 17-30.

Router Configuration

Say you're asked to make 8 subnets viable with the subnet mask 255.255.255.224 in Class C. What do you think should the router configuration command be?

Choices:

A. Router Config #ip Classless

B. Router Config #no ip Classful

C. Router Config #ip unnumbered

D. Router Config #ip subnet-zero

Answer

For this, the answer is D because there are 3 bits on the subnet mask 255.255.255.224, that also has 5 bits off and works with 30 hosts.

Take note though that you might only be using 6 subnets here, not considering subnet zero.

Chapter 9: Subnetting Practice Questions

2-Subnet Network

Look at the illustration below and you'll see that one of the devices on the given network has been disfigured.

The question now is which of the devices has an invalid IP Address?

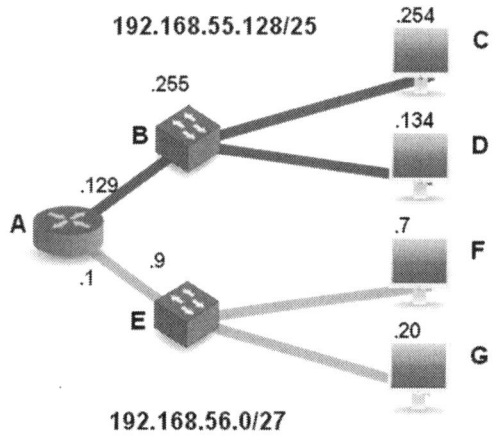

Answer

For this, the answer is B.

In order to figure this out, you have to make sure that you find the right block size, and to determine that all devices and networks fall on the said block size—otherwise, it would be invalid.

You also should check whether network and broadcast addresses are assigned to the hosts. Keep in mind that the usable hosts are those that are between the network and the broadcast address.

Subnets and Hosts per Subnets 1

This is a three-part test (just like the two more succeeding ones). Check it out below:

1. If your network is 192.161.204.0, how many subnets and hosts per subnet could you get from it?

2. If your network is 192.16.21.0 255.255.255.128, how many subnets and hosts per subnet could you get from it?

3. If your network is 192.16.21.0 255.255.255.128, how many subnets and hosts per subnet could you get from it?

Answer

What you need to do here is remember that you need to find a singular subnet mask. This way, you'd get around 1000 subnets with 50 hosts each and VLSM would be involved.

Class B is the given address, with bits that are borrowed from the 3rd to the 4th octet. This way, you could create 1000 subnets.

Now, go ahead and calculate the power of two that could be returned greater than normal value of 1000. For this, it would be 10.

This means:

$$2^{\wedge}10 = 1024$$

1 2 3 4 5 6 7 8 9 10

11

2 4 6 8 16 32 64 128 256 512 1024 2-48

Therefore, the subnet mask for this question is /26 or 255.255.255.192, which means you have 6 remaining hosts that could reach up to 64, and that you have 62 valid hosts for each subnet.

Network, Broadcast Address, First and Last IP

1. If the host is 172.30.11.15/26, then what is the Network ID, Broadcast Address, and the first and last IP?

2. If the host is 172.19.0.0 255.255.254.0, what is the Network ID, Broadcast Address, and the first and last IP?

3. If 192.168.1.1 is the host, what is the Network ID, Broadcast Address, as well as the first and last IP?

Answer

For this, what you can do is check out the network mask. You'll see that the 4th octet has 224 on it so that it could borrow bits until it reaches what it needs to reach. To figure out how many bits have been borrowed, you should make a list like the one shown below:

128 84 32 16 8 4 2 1

1 1 1 0 0 0 0 0

This means that 3-bits have already been found for the subnets and that there are 5 bits that are still remaining for each of the hosts. This means that $2 \wedge 3 = 8$, and $2 \wedge 5 = 32$, which states that you have 8 subnets and 32 hosts.

Subnet Belonging

If 192.168.137.249 is the network, then to which subnet does it belong to?

Answer

The network belongs to 192.168.137.192.

Maximum Number of Subnets

Suppose the network is 172.28.0.0/22, what do you think is the maximum number of valid subnets, as well as the number of hosts per subnet?

Answer

For this question, the answer is that you have 1024 subnets that contain 62 hosts each.

Shorthand Mask

If the subnet mask is 255.255.128.0, what is its corresponding shorthand mask?

Answer

The shorthand mask is /17.

Broadcast Address for Network

If the network address is 172.17.168.40 255.255.255.248, what do you think is the broadcast address?

Answer

For the given example, the broadcast address would be 172.17.168.47.

Designing Network Plan

Suppose you were asked to design an address plan for the network 172.16.0.0. You were also told that your company needs 1500 subnets that contain 50 hosts per subnet. What do you think should the appropriate subnet mask is?

Answer

For this one, the appropriate subnet mask is 255.255.255.224 or /27.

Last Valid Host

If the host is 172.19.192.206, what do you think is the last valid host on the said network?

Answer

The last valid host on this network is 172.19.197.206

Subnet Host

If the network is 10.154.124.201 255.255.252.0, in which subnet mask does it belong to?

Answer

For this one, the answer is 10.154.124.0

Designing Address Plan

Your network is 172.16.0.0. What do you think is the address plan that could accommodate the said network that would be able to fit in 400 subnets that contain 70 hosts per subnet. Now, the question is, which subnet mask should you use?

Answer

For this one, the appropriate mask is 255.255.255.128 or /25.

Last Valid Host

If the network is 172.22.126.53/22, what do you think is the last valid host?

Answer

For this one, you have to make sure that you find the succeeding block and that you subtract 2 from the said block. Again, the last usable IP would be the one that's one less than the given broadcast, which means that the answer to this question is 172.22.127.254.

VLAN Subnet Masks

Suppose you have 21 hosts in VLAN A with the address 192.168.143.24, and you have 23 hosts in VLAN B with network 192.168.143.57. What do you think is the subnet mask that has been used for the network?

Answer

The subnet mask that is appropriate for the given networks is 255.255.255.224.

Three Subnetworks

Suppose your subnetwork is 192.168.17.0/24 and that it has been divided into subnet A and B, but you were asked to create a third subset that contains 16 hosts.

The question is: Do you think that this is a viable request and that it is possible, and if yes, what do you think is the network address of this new subnet? If it is not possible, justify why "no" is your answer.

Answer

The answer is that it is possible.

To figure this out, you have to calculate the space that A and B subnets take up, and for this, you have to look at the network mask. Now, you have to start working from the last octet by subtracting the value of the network mask from the final octet (octet 256). This way, you would be able to figure out how many IP addresses the subnet masks use.

So, for subnet A, you could conclude that 256-192 will give you 64 addresses, and same goes for B, which will also give you 64 IPS.

Now, you have to figure out how many of these IPs do you really need, which means that you would need 16 hosts. Find the block size and subtract 2 to figure out how many IPs you need—now, you could use 32 addresses.

Therefore, the answer is 192.168.17.128 because it is the first IP used in the next block that is also a net mask of subnet B.

Choose the Valid Host

Among the choices below, choose the valid IP Host if the network is 191.254.0.0, and that you have to use 11 bits while subnetting:

191.254.0.96

191.254.0.32

191.254.1.29

191.54.1.64

Answer

The correct answer here is 191.254.1.29 because your Class B Network Address has a default subnet mask of 255.255.255.0. This means to create 16-bit yields, you have to add 11 subnetting bits, and then soon enough, your yield may reach 27. Now, you would be able to create the new mask of 255.255.255.224.

Convert 255.255.255.224 to binary and then convert the lowest subnet to decimal.

You should then see that the lowest order non-zero bit is 32, with the same decimal value, and that this is also used as interval for the next subnets. The first 10 subnets should also give you the right IP Range.

For this, you should have the following:

192.254.0.191.254.0.1 -191.254.0.30

191.254.0.32.191.254.0.33 − 191.254.0.62

191.254.0.32.191.254.65 - 191.254.0.94

And so on until you reach

191.254.1.32.191.254.1.33 – 191.254.1.62

These means that the given addresses also work as subnets—but only in this given scenario. 11 bits of subnetting should always be used for equations like this one.

Large Corporation

Suppose that you're working for this large corporation that's said to be a Class A Network. There are currently 1000 subnets in the company and you're asked to add 100 more subnets over the next three years. You also should be able to have the largest amount of hosts per subnet.

The question is, which subnet mask should you choose and use?

Answer

Basically, what you have to do here is add 100 subnets to 1000 subnets. Of course, this would give you 1,100 subnets which could tell you that there could be thousands of available hosts.

Now, you should raise 2 to the power of 10 and then subtract 2. This would give you 1022 since 1024 is the main answer, and you always have to subtract 2 from it. Borrow another host bit and raise 2 to the power of 11, subtract 2, and multiply the answer by 2.

This means that you'd have 2046 useful subnets.

Take note that:

> 11111111.00000000.00000000.0000000 0 will give you Class A Subnet Mask with 255.0.0.0

> 11111111.11111111.11100000.00000000 will give you Class A Subnet Mask with 255.255.224.0 and 11 bits of subnetting

Subnet Requirements

Lastly, suppose your company's Network ID is 165.121.0.0 and you're asked to create the subnets for the given network, and that those subnets should have 900 host IDs.

Now, the question is: what do you think is the subnet mask that will be able to meet the requirement for the minimum host IDs but would give quality number of subnets?

Answer

For this one, the answer is 255.255.252.0 or Class B Network. This is because it creates around 126 subnets, and if you add 1 to the first 6 digits of the octet, you'll be able to gain more than 510 hosts—you could double the number, which would be more than the 900 requirement, and that's okay.

Now, take note that the least possible IDs range from 00000001 to 11111110, and once converted, it could reach 3.254 so you could get a range of 165.121.0.1 to 165.121.3.254.

Conclusion

Thank you for reading this book!

Hopefully, this book was able to help you to understand Subnetting and that you're now prepared for your review.

Finally, if you enjoyed this book, please take time to post a review on Amazon. It will be greatly appreciated.

Thank you and good luck!

Made in the USA
Middletown, DE
02 June 2016